The Sawtooth Mountain Dream

Running Redfish Lake Lodge

Kelsey Newman Benac

THE SAWTOOTH MOUNTAIN DREAM by KELSEY NEWMAN BENAC

First Edition

ISBN: 978-0-578-02792-0

Table of Contents

Author's Note

At the Redfish Lake Lodge office, we often receive correspondence from reflective patrons and former employees expressing great affection for their time spent at Redfish Lake. One former employee shares, "I worked in the Redfish Lake Lodge store during the summer of 1982, and it was one of the best times of my life. I had never been to Redfish or Stanley before that, and ever since then I've had a burning desire to return."[1] A patron reveals, "Some of my fondest memories are the times I spent at Redfish. I tell my 5-year-old daughter [. . .] stories all the time about your breathtaking location. Sometimes when we go to sleep at night she tells me that she's going to her happy place, Redfish Lake. Life has taken me [elsewhere], but my heart will always be in Idaho."[2]

My own affection for the region began when I was a child. My fondest memories are family vacations and girls camp adventures to the Sawtooths nearly every summer of my youth. Many years after my childhood, I found myself working in the corporate world, feeling harried and much too far removed from my rural Idaho roots. It was time to reevaluate, so I quit my job and called Jeff Clegg about a Human Resources position open at Redfish Lake Lodge. I wanted to return to the magical place of my childhood. Jeff offered me the job. I wholeheartedly accepted.

I worked for the lodge from 2001 to 2004, two years longer than I expected, but it's a hard place to leave. Even now I experience pangs of nostalgia for the four summers I spent working there. It is truly an enchanted region, and it has cast its spell on many. Why the enchantment? Why the fuss? Well, there are no words to adequately answer "why," but the answer is obvious to anyone who walks the shores of Redfish Lake. There are words to answer "how," and that is the purpose of this book: to explore the development of Redfish Lake and, more specifically, Redfish Lake Lodge.

My research is not exhaustive, and it often relies on memories that in some cases are more than 50 years old. The limitations are obvious, and though I have tried to be thorough in my research, and thus to write as accurate a representation as possible, I am keenly aware of the potential for error or misinterpretation. I must also note that I never tracked down any legal documents regarding ownership transactions, other than a copy of a lease and agreement between Dick Horstman and Bob Limbert. When I contacted Custer County about such records, they referred me to the US Forest Service, and when I contacted the Forest Service, they referred me to Custer County. I traveled this circle a few times before I decided to forgo the exact legal details and instead rely on verbal accounts.

I hope that through reader feedback and continued research, the history of Redfish Lake Lodge can be expanded and revised. If you have any photographs or memories of the lodge or Redfish Lake and you would like to contribute to the historical file, then please do! You can send email to history@redfishlake.com, or mail to Redfish Lake Lodge, PO Box 43, Jerome, ID 83338.

Many thanks to everyone who has already willing shared their memories with me, and many thanks to those who will!

Kelsey Newman Benac

Redfish Lake Lodge, 2004

Redfish Lake Lodge resort map, 2002

Introduction

In central Idaho rises a mountain range supreme in its ability to captivate a heart and command an audience. These wild, striking, and saw-like peaks are aptly called the Sawtooth Mountains. Throughout the ages, glaciers cut and carved the granite masses of the Idaho and Sawtooth Batholiths, leaving the jagged peaks, deep glaciated valleys, and the glittering glacial lakes of the Sawtooth Region. Redfish Lake is the largest of these in the region and is often referred to as the "jewel of the Sawtooths."

This glacial lake stretches north five miles from the bases of Grand Mogul and Mt. Heyburn. Sandy beaches frame its northern end. Crystal clear, blue waters reach depths of 387 feet, and temperatures range from freezing in winter months to around 60 degrees Fahrenheit in July and August. Until recent years, hordes of salmon migrated to and from Redfish Lake, inspiring its name because of the bright red color they take on when spawning. Though once thick with these fish, by the late decades of the 20th century over-fishing and developments such as dams endangered the salmon populations until virtually none returned. Now efforts are underway to rehabilitate these fish populations.

The earliest human visitors to this country were prehistoric hunters and later Native American tribes. They came to Sawtooth valleys in the summers to fish and hunt but generally avoided the inhospitable peaks of the surrounding mountains. Few Native Americans actually lived in the area because of the harsh winters with sub-zero temperatures and deep snow, although by the 1800s one band of Shoshone called the Sheepeaters did inhabit the valley. Early settlers in the valley recalled that Native Americans relied on the red fish of mountain lakes as a food source.[3]

Euro-Americans arrived in the Sawtooth Valley in the early nineteenth century. Fur trappers were the first to venture into the region, followed by prospectors after the discovery of gold in the 1860s. Boomtowns such as Bonanza City, Custer, and Sawtooth City prospered for a few decades. The city of Stanley endured as the commercial hub of the region with a focus on cattle ranching and trade. Reports in local newspapers suggest that these regional settlers visited Redfish Lake for abundant supplies of fish and presumably for recreation as well; however, there is no indication of permanent settlement at the lake during the nineteenth century.

Though relatively unaffected by the regional settlement and development of the nineteenth century, Redfish Lake did gain popularity as a recreation destination and at times a commercial destination. In 1882, Mrs. W.H. Broadhead explained, "Already [the lake] is a favorite resort for those who know of its attractions."[4] Wood River Valley residents provided an "annual string of excursionists" that spent days in July and August camping and fishing on the shores of Redfish Lake, and entrepreneurs frequented the lake for commercial gain, harvesting fish to sell to local hotels and restaurants. Some pondered the possibilities of developing canneries and fish traps at the lake, but none came to fruition and later laws prohibited fish trapping and deterred such commercial development.[5]

In 1905 President Teddy Roosevelt created the Sawtooth Forest Reserve, which was later renamed the Sawtooth National Forest. The reserve included Redfish Lake and placed its shores under the administration of the U.S. Forest Service. The Forest Service began building trails, campgrounds, and picnic areas around the lake. Increasingly, the area seemed destined for recreational development. Indeed, the Forest Service deemed scenic and recreational values the most important considerations in land-use decisions involving the Redfish Lake area.

Social and industrial developments of the early 20th century allowed average Americans the opportunity to visit the region and revel in its natural beauty. With the advent of the automobile, Americans began traveling in unprecedented numbers and, not surprisingly, the Sawtooth region was discovered as a premier destination. The momentum of tourism began.

Edith Robertson at Redfish Lake, c1920
Courtesy Edith Robertson

The first significant waves of tourists arrived after highway construction projects in 1920 and 1927 improved the road over Galena and through the Stanley Basin, thus permitting automobile travel to the region. Early auto tourist Peter Ball marveled as he passed over Galena and caught his first glimpse of "the earth stand[ing] on end." He describes this encounter with the Sawtooths as "an exotic spectacle as the sharp fingers of these ragged mountains offered themselves in their most romantic mood, with the sun setting behind them. Time, place, everything but the great peak ceased to exist. Life at that moment had reached one of those rare points with which it is so frugal."[6] His amazement and appreciation is echoed in sentiments from countless visitors who have followed.

Entrepreneurs immediately recognized the potential for tourism and considered Redfish Lake one of the "the most desirable location[s]" for such development.[7] The Occupancy Act of 1915 allowed 30-year special use permits for private commercial development at the lake, and Dick Horstman developed the first lodging and boating concessions at Redfish Lake in the early 1920s. Within several years Bob Limbert partnered with him to remodel and expand facilities at the lake. Failing health forced Horstman out of the venture around 1928 and Limbert assumed responsibility, spending the next five years developing what we know today as Redfish Lake Lodge. Tragically, Limbert suffered a premature and sudden death from a heart attack in June 1933. The resort passed into the hands of manager George S. Krom, but virtually nothing is known about his ownership.

Tourism slowed with the Depression and the Second World War. Little development happened from 1933 to 1946, and Redfish Lake Lodge was closed much of that time.[8] After the war ended, tourism picked up in earnest. Road construction projects throughout the 1950s and 1960s improved accessibility, and with every improvement, came new waves of tourists. The state oiled the highway over Galena in the 1950s, and the completion of Highway 21 in the 1960s connected the Boise area to the region. Tourism increased hand in hand with accessibility, and facilities at Redfish Lake strained to keep up with demand. The Forest Service expanded camping facilities around the lake, and each successive Redfish Lake Lodge owner from 1960 forward has expanded the resort to accommodate the needs of thousands of tourists who now visit each summer.

What started as a small two-story hotel in the early 1920s grew into a 16.8 acre resort with diverse amenities. Today its features include the lodge, rental cabins, a restaurant and bar, a marina, a store, a service station, horse corrals, public showers and public laundry, and employee housing.[9]

Redfish Lake Lodge has been owned by the following parties over the years:

1920-1927	Bernard D. Horstman
1927-1933	Robert W. Limbert
1933-unknown[10]	George S. Krom
1946-1954	Jess Worthington and Roy Butcher
1954-1960	Pret Maughan and Loran Olson families
1960-1971	Redfish Lake Enterprises
1972-1998	Donald and Correen See family
1999-present (2009)	Arlen and Derrel Crouch

The chapters of this book examine the experience of each ownership and its specific contributions to Redfish Lake Lodge.

Bernard D. Horstman
1920-1927

German immigrant Bernard D. (Dick) Horstman began homesteading near Redfish Lake in the early 1900s. In 1920 he received a permit from the Forest Service to move operations to the northern shore of Redfish Lake where he pursued tourism instead of agriculture. Horstman built a hotel and boating concession and became the first known resort concessionaire at Redfish Lake.[11] In addition to the hotel and boat piers, Horstman constructed an ice house, boat house, store house, and personal dwelling cabin.

There is little recorded history about Horstman's operation at Redfish and few recollections. Jack See recounts a humorous memory from Alta Ellis about a distinctive breakfast with Horstman:

> She told a story that they used to come to Redfish when Horstman ran the lodge. Dick was a bachelor and she said they'd go out and have his sourdough pancakes on Sunday morning with her dad. Alta [remarked], "Oh, you put raisins in the pancakes?"... Dick replied, "Raisins? No, those are horseflies."[12]

Esther Yarber recalled Horstman hiring local Stanley Basin resident Leafy Critchfield to manage the resort one summer. When his health began failing, Horstman hired a Mr. Kerr to run the business.[13]

Photographs from the time depict tourist activity at the lake. Edna McGown reported: "It was probably in the early '20s [1920s] that people really started to come into the country just for sightseeing and camping, fishing, and that sort of thing, because of the cars. They could travel easier and longer distances."[14] It follows that demand for facilities and services such as the Lake Hotel and boat rentals increased too; however, it appears that Horstman did not have the health or funds to keep up with demand.

Various accounts reference Horstman's failing health, and letters in the Robert W. Limbert Collection suggest that Horstman may not have had the funds to improve the resort as needed. The District Forester at the time expressed a "desire to see a strong organization with ample finances undertake the development of hotel and resorts in this section,"[15] but Horstman's facilities, as described by Bob Limbert, were "not of much account, crude, small and cramped."[16]

By 1927, Horstman had signed over his lease on the Redfish properties to Limbert. Initially Horstman remained connected to the business through his boating concession, but by 1929 he sold that to Limbert as well, and Limbert entered the scene with the passion and financial backing to develop a "dude ranch," which he "intended to be the last word in camps of [its] kind."[17]

Robert W. Limbert
1927 - 1933

Robert (Bob) Limbert is something of an Idaho history celebrity and one of the most notable promoters of tourism in the Sawtooths. He moved from Nebraska to Boise, Idaho, in 1911 at age 26. He quickly began championing his new home state, and in 1915 he designed an award-winning exhibition about Idaho for the Pan-Pacific International Exposition. He also began exploring regions such as the lava fields of south-central Idaho and the Bruneau River region. He wrote many articles about his explorations for national publications, one of which brought attention to and ultimately National Monument designation for Craters of the Moon. Though he loved and explored all of southern Idaho, he settled and invested in the Sawtooth Region.

In 1926 he and six other men formed Sawtooth Tours Inc. to develop tourism in the Hailey-Sawtooth district.[18] Jostling with other developers and investors, the company proposed lodges and camps at lakes throughout the Sawtooths. In a 1928 letter to investor Lewis Megowen of Chicago, Limbert warns of "about thirty applications from people who want to install everything from hamburger stands to real investment" at Stanley Lake.[19] Limbert competed heartily with the many applicants, and he eventually partnered with Horstman to purchase his lease at Redfish Lake. In November of 1927, the two men entered a contract wherein Limbert assumed the lease on all buildings and holdings at Redfish Lake, except the boating concession and Horstman's personal cabin, which Horstman retained until 1929.

Limbert moved his family to Redfish Lake in 1928 to begin construction on facilities that he modeled after such establishments as Yellowstone National Park and Jackson Hole. With the financial backing of Chicago contacts Lewis Megowen and J.L.

Kraft, he began an addition to the existing Lake Hotel. Limbert envisioned a two-story, log-cabin style lodge, which included a dining room and lobby on the lower level and rental rooms on the upper level. Upon seeing photographs of the remodeling project, Megowen and Kraft felt the lodge needed to be bigger to accommodate more guests. Megowen's father was a retired engineer and building contractor, and he drew up plans that required tearing down the Lake Hotel and extending the lodge 40 feet west.[20] In addition to the lodge construction, Limbert installed canvas tent cabins for additional rental units, again replicating facilities at Yellowstone, and he built a convenience store and gas station. The undertaking was overwhelming. He wrote to a friend, "As for me I am so busy I hardly know which thing to do first. Got two crews of men logging and three carpenters working and two guys swinging a shovel. Hot diggety."[21]

Bob Limbert
Courtesy Boise State University Special Collections: Robert W. Limbert Collection

Construction crews harvested logs and floated them from the head of the lake to the building site; carpenters worked on the lodge; Limbert worked on projects such as ordering mattresses, painting dining room tables, and coordinating with the Forest Service to install a transmitter and batteries. By the fall of 1928, crews had logs for the lodge laid higher than

Limbert's head, the gas station finished, and the store started. Construction closed down during the harsh winter months, and Limbert spent his time traveling and promoting Redfish, leaving his properties in the hands of caretaker Trapper Green.

Upon returning the following year, Limbert described the condition of the resort:

> We have enough logs cut to finish all necessary construction work, the gasoline station building is finished all but the roof and flooring, a store building 16x24 inside measurement is up ready for roofing. The hotel building has the dining room and kitchen completed and the walls of the rest of the building up ready to put the roof and upper part of the second floor on.
>
> The ice house, boat house, a building about 20x32 in size and the store house are finished. These are the old buildings which were finished when I took over. The boat docks are completed all but planking the tops which should done [*sic*] as the tops at present are made of logs and poles. There are two motor boats.
>
> To put the place in running order the hotel building must be completed and furnished. The stove, dishes, silver wear, etc. are all on hand. I also have eight tent cabins completed and materials for two more on hand.
>
> Water will have to be piped about 150 yards and proper plumbing installed. I estimate and have had others tell me the same thing that it will take about $15,000 to finish the place up in first class shape.[22]

Shortly after this assessment, Limbert faced a major setback when Megowen, his principal financial backer, went broke in the spring of 1929. With his resort two-thirds done and without the money to finish, he felt "left away out on the end of a branch and the branch about half sawed in two."[23] He scrambled to find other investors and persevered to end the summer of 1929 in partial operation: he notes in a letter that the dining room and boat dock had been operating all summer; and he had eight finished tent cabins.[24]

Though his first years of operation coincided with the onset of the Great Depression, Limbert managed to achieve full operation by drawing upon proceeds from his winter performances and mortgaging his assets. By 1931, he completed the lodge, 10 tent cabins, three duplex log cabins (which are the present day Rustic Cabins), a convenience store, gas station, and shower house. He also improved upon the existing docks, store house, boat house, and ice house. Redfish Lake Lodge was on its way to becoming a legendary vacation spot and received its share of guests.

Limbert's daughter, Margaret Lawrence, recalls jovial evening campfires on the beach in front of the lodge where everyone gathered to enjoy the music of harmonicas, ukuleles, accordions, and guitars. Limbert looked for musical ability when he hired help: he wanted entertainers. They sang songs, told stories, and enjoyed the friendly campfire atmosphere, and people came from all the nearby campgrounds to join in the merriment. She remembers guests coming to hunt and ride horses.[25] Her father would take the men out hunting, and "they'd pretend like they shot something, but my dad always told how he shot it."[26] She remembers her mother serving milkshakes and banana splits in the restaurant, as well as freshly caught fish from the lake. They also served wild game like deer and elk.

Lawrence has particularly fond memories of an old "Packard" boat that could hold 22 people. Nobody but her father was allowed to drive the boat. It had a Packard motor, which was significant at the time because Packard cars were considered trustworthy, so the name gave people confidence. She remembers her father using the boat to rescue and tow in other boaters when storms came up on the lake. Another prominent memory for her was the green glassware in the dining room. Her father catered to wealthy clients who liked fine things, and he liked green, so he served up their cuisine on the finest green glassware.

Limbert, his wife, and four children lived in one of the tent cabins during the summers, and Lawrence remembers having a good life there and creating some of the happiest memories of her life. Sadly, tragedy struck just a few years into this venture. In June of 1933, Limbert was traveling back from Chicago to be with his dying mother in Boise. En route, he himself died of a heart attack at 48 years of age.[27] His tragic and premature death left his family devastated, and his business was soon insolvent. Lawrence said, "After dad died, we lost everything."[28]

Limbert's untimely death prevented the influence he might have had on further developments in the broad Sawtooth region, but it did not end his influence at Redfish Lake Lodge. The resort expanded much in the following 80 years, but as of 2009 it still operates with the same basic structure established by Limbert, and most of the original buildings are still used on the property, whether in original or altered form. Limbert's legacy is very much alive.

George S. Krom
1933 - unknown

The status of Redfish Lake Lodge in the years following Limbert's death is a bit of a mystery. Forest Service records indicate the lodge passing to George S. Krom, who is also noted on a 1931 Redfish Lake Lodge brochure as the reservation contact and manager for Sawtooth Hotels & Tours.[29] It seems that Krom had a management role in the resort and Sawtooth Tours, Inc., the company founded by Limbert and six others in 1926. Limbert explained to an investor that he preferred to focus on publicity and field operation, rather than daily management.[30] Perhaps Krom filled the role of day-to-day manager. Krom is again mentioned on a Redfish Lake Lodge brochure, which presumably dates between 1933 and 1941, but this time his name is listed without specific title. He is noted as the information and reservation contact, and the winter address is listed as 151 East 80th St., N.Y.C. Limbert had many connections in the East and solicited the financial investment of Eastern moguls, so perhaps Krom was one of the Eastern investors or an associate. There is no record of how long Krom operated the lodge; a Forest Service report cites various unknown investors after Limbert's death.[31] Other accounts suggest that the lodge reverted back to Horstman's estate and that Horstman's heirs chose to close the lodge but continue boat rentals until their Forest Service lease expired in 1942.[32]

Though the ownership and the operating status of the lodge are vague, vacationers continued to enjoy Redfish Lake. Emmett Hood shared a photograph from a summer visit in 1935. In it his family is posed in front of the lodge, but the lodge is boarded shut and obviously closed. ``Idaho, A Guide in Word and Pictures," which was published in 1937, states, "the hotel and cabins on Big Redfish have never been opened (for reasons which seem quite mysterious), but boats can be rented and campsites are many."[33] Photographs from 1939 also depict boating and fishing on the lake, and perhaps the store was open as well. Additionally, from 1937 to 1940 a Civilian Conservation Corps unit of 75 men was stationed at Redfish Lake to construct infrastructure such as roads, campgrounds, bridges, and telephone lines.[34]

Jack Niece, a lifelong Stanley resident, remembers going to Redfish Lake in 1937 to watch a forest fire at the upper west side of the lake, but he doesn't remember any details about lodge operations other than it being open intermittently between 1933 and 1942.[35] The lodge was closed during World War II and suffered from neglect and vandalism. Rocks had been thrown through windows and boats were punctured. In 1946, the lodge reopened but was in desperate need of repair. Fortunately, new owners Jess Worthington and Roy Butcher came onto the scene with the financial resources necessary to get the resort up and running in time for the tourism boom that followed World War II.

Worthington & Butcher
1946 - 1953

After suffering vandalism and disrepair during its closure for World War II, Redfish Lake Lodge was in desperate need of attention. In 1946 it reopened under the new ownership of Jess Worthington and Roy Butcher, who had the financial means to mend and recondition the resort as necessary. Worthington hailed from San Diego, California, and Butcher was from San Jose, California. Worthington was an Idaho native who grew up in the Twin Falls area and kept a home there to which he frequently returned even after moving to California.[36] His love of hunting, fishing, and the Idaho outdoors must have provided the impetus for purchasing Redfish Lake Lodge.

It seems that Worthington and Butcher envisioned the lodge as a type of business and personal retreat. They came, along with friends and associates from California, to escape the city and play in the mountains. Irene Wells Burr, a Stanley resident who worked for them at the lodge, describes them as nice people but different from the Stanley population, because they were "rich city folk." She remembers them hosting big, lavish parties that were "pretty shocking" to a self-described small-town, Idaho girl.[37]

Worthington and Butcher hired managers to run the resort rather than living and working there themselves. The first summer they hired Roy and Helen Frizzelle from Twin Falls to manage and revive the lodge. Their daughter, Kelly Yost, recalls that the object was to get the resort in running condition, rather than to have guests; and indeed, there were some guests, but not many. Most time and effort was poured into replacing broken boats and windows, painting, installing a generator and repairing electrical wiring, pouring cement, and other general repairs.

Worthington and Butcher operated the lodge in a somewhat exclusive fashion. The dining room served only lodging guests as opposed to the general public, and meals were served at specific times. Loran Olson described the atmosphere as "dress for dinner." The convenience store and docks, on the other hand, remained open to the public.[38]

Jess Worthington
Courtesy Kelly Yost

In 1947 an unidentified couple managed the lodge. That same year Jewell Campbell and her brother Dee stopped at Redfish on a trip from southern California. They ended up staying to work for the summer and Jewell Campbell so impressed the owners that they offered her the manager position for the following summer. Campbell managed the resort for two summers before marrying and moving away with local forest ranger Dean Rowland. However, she was prevailed upon to finish out seasons in 1950 and 1952 when other managers either quit or were fired.[39]

By 1953 Worthington and Butcher were ready to sell, perhaps because of the difficulties of running the business from a distance, especially without the support of reliable managers. Loran Olson suggested, moreover, that relations between Worthington and Butcher and the Forest Service were strained because of differing visions for the resort.

For example, the Forest Service wanted dining services available to the public, rather than limited to lodging guests. Paul B. Larson of Boise was enlisted as the real estate agent for the sale, and Pret Maughan and family members subsequently purchased Redfish Lake Lodge.

Maughan & Olson
1953 - 1960

In 1953 Pret Maughan and his wife Sally had just purchased a new home in Twin Falls where he worked as a Snap-on Tool salesman for the Twin Falls/Boise district. He also owned the Crooked Bar on Broadway Avenue in Boise. Sally's brother Loran Olson and his wife Helen were farmers in the Boise area. But all of this changed after Boise contractor and real estate agent Paul B. Larson approached Pret Maughan about purchasing Redfish Lake Lodge.

Pret and Sally liked the idea of owning and operating the lodge, and they decided to invite Loran and Helen Olson to partner with them. At the time the Olsons' milk cows were inexplicably drying up, and consequently so was their income. Loran remembers "shoveling ditch" one day, mulling over his frustrating situation when Pret and Sally showed up with a proposition. At first Loran offered to put money in the deal, but he didn't want to go up to Redfish: "We was [*sic*] just ol' farmers. We didn't know nothing [*sic*] about working with people."[40] But he had second thoughts after considering his financial situation: no milk check, no income. He and Helen decided to team up with the Maughans. Another couple, Jay and Pearl Gorton, joined as well. Pret and Sally sold the Crooked Bar and their new home as a down payment for the lodge, and thus in 1954, the three couples embarked on a new business venture together.

The tradition of family business began with the Maughan and Olson ownership. For six summers they "worked [themselves] to death," as they later described it, to keep the resort running. Under their stewardship the ambiance quickly changed from what Loran Olson described as the "dress for dinner" tone of the previous owners to a "come as you are," family-friendly approach.[41] They had no experience running a lodging operation. They learned by experience and discovered that it was hard work. They hired one or two employees to help in the kitchen and dining room but did everything else themselves, working seven days a week throughout the season. Within the first summer, the Gortons decided it was not what they had bargained for and left, leaving the Maughans and Olsons as the owners and operators.

One of their first objectives was to restore public access to the dining room, a move much favored by the Forest Service. Maughan and Olson opened the dining room to serve meals all day, and they even built a counter in the kitchen where guests could order their food and chat with the cook while it was prepared.

They built a new horse corral, and they rewired the lodge to connect to a new government power line. Previously the lodge relied on a generator for electricity, but in early 1954 the Forest Service brought a power line to the lodge, and Loran became a self-taught electrician when he wired the lodge to connect to the power line, rather than the generator. During the course of their ownership, Maughan and Olson faced increasing demand to expand facilities and contemplated other improvements such as new cabins and trailer spaces; however, they lacked the financial resources for such expansion and instead focused on maintaining and improving the existing services and facilities.

Running the lodge was definitely a family affair. The two couples had four children between them, and the kids were often enlisted to clean cabins and wash dishes when necessary. These four young cousins also proved to be budding entrepreneurs, cleaning guests' fish for a fee and collecting moss-covered limbs to sell to tourists. The adults did not officially divide job responsibilities, but rather jumped in wherever needed. As an example, Helen explains guest registration: "The office [was] a little corner in the lobby where we kept the registration book, and that was like everything else, whoever was handy registered people."[42]

They remember working long, hard hours and hardly noticing the lake. Sally recalls one visitor commenting, "Boy you sure got a beautiful place here. I bet you sure enjoy the lake." Sally responds, "We were so busy that we didn't have time to know there was a lake there, let alone enjoy it." Another guest commented to Helen that they ought to run a place like Redfish Lake Lodge in Florida in the wintertime, to which Helen shot back, "Do you want us to go crazy?!"[43] The two women spent every day of the summer cleaning, cooking, and serving the guests from sun up to sun down. Pret and Loran would leave the property to go to Boise to get supplies, but Helen recalls that she and Sally spent the whole summer right at the lodge.

Their guests came from all over, even as far away as Europe: Sally specifically remembers a couple visiting from France. During the day, guests rented boats, rode horses, or geared up with fishing supplies from the store. At night they relaxed in front of the fireplace in the lodge lobby (which Redfish Lake Enterprises later converted into the Rustic Lounge). Families would spend their evenings in front of the lounge fireplace reading or playing games, and the Maughans and Olsons took pride in this family-friendly atmosphere. In fact, when the Forest Service suggested that they convert the lobby and lounge area to a bar, they resolutely declined because they did not want to jeopardize the family traditions.

The Forest Service's suggestion for a bar was likely in response to the popular demand of an ever increasing number of tourists. As the numbers of visitors continued to soar throughout the 1950s, various expansions and changes were necessary to accommodate the increasing traffic at Redfish Lake. The Forest Service drafted a plan that included, among other things, a 20-space trailer court expansion at Redfish Lake Lodge.[44]

Near the end of the Maughan and Olson tenure, the Forest Service increased pressure on them to either expand or sell. Because the existing facilities could not handle the demand, another party began petitioning the Forest Service for a permit to open a new commercial establishment on the lake. The Forest Service told Maughan and Olson that if they would agree to sell the lodge to someone with greater financial resources, then the Forest Service would be able to reject the petition for additional building at Redfish Lake. Maughan and Olson lacked the capital to expand their operation. They had exhausted their energies and resources just to keep the lodge running, and even had to work other jobs in the winters to make ends meet. Additionally, as their children got older, it became more difficult to move twice a year and juggle school schedules. It seemed time to move on, and so in 1959, after selling the lodge to Redfish Lake Enterprises, both families returned to settle in the Boise area.

Helen Olson, Pearl Gorton, and Sally Maughan in the dining room, 1954
Courtesy Sally Maughan

Redfish Lake Enterprises
1960 - 1972

By 1959 Redfish Lake facilities were overloaded. The Forest Service was working to expand camping and picnic facilities and was also anxious to enlist an owner that could increase Redfish Lake Lodge capacity. After Maughan and Olson put the lodge on the market, Bob Coiner of Twin Falls, Idaho, heard about the opportunity and began to organize a company to purchase the lodge. Fellow Twin Falls residents Ken Brown, Bob Tucker, and Mel Jensen joined Coiner to create Redfish Lake Enterprises as the original shareholders; however, Brown shortly left the venture and sold his shares to Art Harshbarger. Redfish Lake Enterprises signed a 20-year lease with the Forest Service and took possession of Redfish Lake Lodge on January 1, 1960.

Bob Tucker acted as the manager. He and Art Harshbarger lived at the resort throughout the summers, while Bob Coiner and Mel Jensen continued their previous business commitments in the Twin Falls area. Coiner and Jensen visited the resort on the weekends to help as needed. This new team immediately embarked on the first major building projects since Limbert's establishment of the resort.

Their initial task was to construct a 40-space trailer court. They spent the first season cutting trailer spaces, digging water lines, and installing septic tanks. Tom Wilkins, an employee at the time, wrote describing the intense manual labor involved in septic installation: "The Forest Service required us to dig a trench by each trailer, approximately 20' long and 2' wide, fill the ditch 2/3rds full with decomposed granite, place perforated sewer pipe the length of the ditch, with an elbow/fitting for a trailer sewer hose, cover it with [decomposed granite] and DONE! You had a sewer!"[45] The required tasks of digging, hauling, and dumping were performed by hand rather than backhoe or tractor-trailer. Once again the operation of Redfish Lake Lodge proved to be hard physical work.

Bob Coiner and Mel Jensen aboard new pontoon boat, 1965
Times-News photo courtesy Mel & Elva Jensen

Running the lodge remained a family affair. Tucker's first wife, Evelyn, ran the store, and later his second wife, Gloria, worked in the kitchen. Betty Coiner remembers working with Marge Brown on projects such as painting rooms. Additionally, each of the owners had teenage children who worked at the lodge. However, as the resort expanded, the owners relied on additional help besides family members. They regularly hired 25 to 30 employees each season, and they faced common challenges with employees. In fact, Betty remembers the help, and specifically kitchen help, as the biggest challenge of the business. One employee got the bar shut down temporarily. At the time, serving liquor on Sundays was prohibited, but a couple of "fellas" sweet-talked one of the female cooks into serving them a drink anyway. It turned out that the sweet-talkers were liquor agents, and they quickly suspended the liquor license for a month. Another time a cook failed to show up for work because of a hangover, and Jensen found himself suddenly cooking breakfast for nearly 100 people.

They faced other challenges as well. Since there were no ice machines then, they had to cut and store 450 tons of ice from the lake in the winter to provide ice to fisherman and campers in the summer. On one winter ice-cutting excursion, Coiner broke through the ice and fell in. "I came out faster than I went in," he said, remembering his reaction to the freezing temperatures.[46] The ice was stored in the ice house, layered between sawdust and plastic sheeting. The ice blocks were about two feet by four feet, and they were cut with a lumber saw into sizes requested by customers. Ice sold for four cents a pound. Wilkins wrote:

> We could usually determine who was from California and who was local by their response to the price! The Californians didn't hesitate paying...not so with the locals! Those that were the most irate were usually offered the opportunity to come up to the lake in April and try their hand at cutting and stacking the ice blocks! (No one was willing to accept!) I remember many of the Californians disbelieving they were actually paying for frozen lake water...until we gave them a tour of the ice house! It was quite the novelty for them then![47]

Though it was difficult to cut and store ice, Jensen says they always had willing help in the wintertime because they turned it into a party, complete with snowmobiles and grilled steaks.

Springtime was challenging as the owners rushed to complete construction projects prior to the summer opening. During the first spring of their ownership, Redfish Lake Enterprises remodeled the lodge by partitioning off the former lobby and creating the bar. They also built a new general store and converted the former Trading Post into the rental cabin now known as the Executive Cabin. Thomas LaMore, who co-managed the resort in 1960, described doing "a year's work this spring."[48] In succeeding years they remodeled the lodge again, adding a lobby and front porch, and they also built the Lodgepole and Pinerest motel units, as well as new public laundry and shower facilities.

Redfish Lake Enterprises also dug a well to replace the existing water supply from a spring on the hill behind the lodge. As guest capacity increased, the spring water supply proved inadequate and was often depleted by 5:30 in the evening. The owners attempted several solutions. First they tried to dig a well at the edge of the hill but ran into granite. They also tried pumping water from the lake but ended up with minnows in their water supply. Finally, they successfully dug a well next to the lodge and replaced the spring-supplied water tank on the hill.

Guests continued to enjoy customary activities like boat rentals, horseback riding, shopping for souvenirs at the general store, and eating in the restaurant. With added attractions by Redfish Lake Enterprises, they could also enjoy things like cocktails in the bar and new paddle boats for playing in the lake. In the evenings, Tucker entertained guests with stories and slide shows of the back country.

Though the families of Redfish Lake Enterprises experienced the typical pleasures and strains of hosting countless guests at the mountain resort, they also experienced a tragedy that overshadowed their ownership. Two boys from the Coiner and Tucker families took a canoe out on the lake one evening in June of 1965, but they never returned. The next morning when staff discovered that Steven Coiner, 16, and Galen Tucker, 17, were missing, the lodge mobilized a rescue effort. Their capsized canoe was found halfway up the lake. Divers later found the boys' bodies.

The accident was a leading factor in selling Redfish Lake Lodge. Bob Coiner understandably explained that Redfish was no longer enjoyable in the way it had been prior to losing his son. Additionally, as the 1960s concluded, the pattern of the previous two decades continued. Tourism was ever-increasing and the partners of Redfish Lake Enterprises felt that someone with more capital would better accommodate the needs of visitors. They listed the resort with LaMoyne Reality, and in 1971 they found a buyer: Donald See and family from southern California.

See Family
1972 - 1999

The year 1972 was a landmark year for Redfish Lake Lodge. It marked the establishment of the Sawtooth National Recreation Area, thus concluding a decades-long land-use debate in which lodge owners had a vested interest. It also marked the beginning of the longest running ownership of Redfish Lake Lodge to date. The See family came in for a "world record [27] seasons" and flavored the resort in ways that became presupposed.

Donald See often visited the Sawtooth Valley from his native southern California to enjoy activities like floating the Middle Fork of the Salmon River and relaxing on the shores of Redfish Lake. During one stay at the lodge in the late 1960s, he was chatting with manager Bob Tucker when he commented, "Gee, I sure love this place." Tucker replied, "How much do you love it?"[49] Apparently he loved it enough, because on January 1, 1972, Donald and Correen See and family took over ownership of the Redfish Lake Lodge resort.

Donald & Correen See

It was a defining time for the resort. The creation of the SNRA would bring more attention to an already popular area, requiring regular expansion and change, and the See family approached expansion with particular vision. They decided that cabins, rather than the trailer court, better suited the long-term image of the resort. They removed the trailer court, and over the course of the next few decades added eight new buildings to the property and remodeled many existing buildings. The general services remained the same, and the whole See family, which included 10 children, worked at the lodge at various times and in varying capacities.

Donald's son and daughter-in-law Jack and Patty had just finished college when he purchased the resort. They had no immediate plans for their life, so when Donald approached them about managing a resort in the Sawtooth Mountains of Idaho, they jumped at the opportunity to "live this mountain dream."[50] Neither had been to Idaho, nor out of California for that matter, except for a summer trip to Ireland. Jack was 22 and Patty was 21. They had little business experience and knew nothing about running a lodge or restaurant, but they did want to live in the mountains of Idaho. Fortunately, according to Jack, the times were "more innocent," and the "business was nothing compared to how busy it is today." This allowed them to grow with the business and as Patty described of their relationship with the resort, "we kind of molded each other."[51] With advice and counsel from Donald, a successful accountant, and his clientele, which included restaurant and hotel owners, Jack and Patty embarked on a long and wonderful relationship with Redfish Lake Lodge.

The Sees had a built-in workforce of family. Three of Don's children and their spouses constituted the management team. Jack and Patty managed the resort throughout the ownership and credit their success to partnership with sister Sharon and brother Daniel. Sharon and her husband Mike Poehling concentrated their efforts managing the front desk and restaurant, all the while raising three daughters. Daniel started working at Redfish in 1972 at the ripe age of 12. Later, he ran the marina and bar operations, while his wife Elizabeth managed the dining room. They had two sons while at Redfish. The other See children worked in various positions, depending on their ages and circumstances.

Left: Patty & Jack See, Right: Mike & Sharon Poehling

Bob Tucker and several cooks from Redfish Lake Enterprises stayed on the first season to help the Sees with the transition. The business required additional staff as well, and like preceding owners, Jack recalls employees being a challenge to the operation. He adopted a "never stop hiring" philosophy because he knew turnover was inevitable, but he always felt fortunate to have good, returning employees in the key positions to help train new staff each season.

The basic services offered at Redfish remained the same, though near-constant infrastructure improvements expanded capacity. One of the See family's significant undertakings was a lodge expansion. They added to the back of the lodge, increasing sleeping capacity upstairs and seating capacity downstairs in the dining room. Throughout the 1970s and 1980s, they engaged in many other improvements as well, building the Deluxe, Getaway, and Fishhook Cabins, as well as the Lake Suites. They also remodeled the Executive Cabin, and reconstructed a cabin for their own personal living quarters. They built the Lake Cabin, which they originally intended as a private cabin for Don and Correen, but before long it entered the rental pool and became one of the most popular family cabins at the resort. Other projects included an addition and remodel to the store, building a new public laundry and shower house, constructing permanent employee housing, and building the open-air gazebo outside the lodge to serve picnic-style lunches.

When the Sees bought the lodge all the plumbing was septic, and the tanks often got overloaded, especially in the spring when melt off would fill the drain fields. Jack recalled pumping gray water into 50-gallon drums at midnight so guests could flush their toilets. In 1972 the Forest Service built the public restroom near the lodge and with it they installed a sewer system connecting from the ranger station. Jack took advantage of this new infrastructure improvement and converted each building's plumbing from the old septic system to the new sewer.

The road structure around the lodge also changed during the See tenure. Previously the turn off to the lodge was by the Redfish Lake Visitor's Center and the road ran in front of the lodge along the beach. In 1979 the road was re-routed to run behind the lodge. This necessitated moving the Lodgepole rental unit and also tearing down half of a shop building to accommodate the new road.

The Sees first considered selling the resort in 1989 and listed it in the Wall Street Journal. According to Don See, it was ``just time to do something else."[52] However, it was a nearly a decade later before negotiations materialized into a deal. In the meantime they did not undertake any major structural changes but maintained the status quo. By 1997 an estimated 1.5 million visited the Sawtooth National Recreation Area annually and Redfish Lake was the most frequented site. In a biological assessment around that time, a Forest Service biologist determined that renewing the permit for Redfish Lake Lodge would jeopardize salmon populations. The Sees had to scientifically refute the claim in order to renew their permit, and thus make the lodge sellable. The Sees prevailed, and in 1997 they were entertaining negotiations for purchase of the lodge from two interested parties: the Crouch family of Jerome, Idaho, and a Colorado company.

Originally, they decided to sell to the Colorado company, but after that deal fell through, they renewed negotiations with the Crouch family. In the fall of 1998, they reached a deal with the Crouches and thus concluded their influential tenure at the resort. Jack and Patty remained in the area, calling Stanley home; Correen survives Don, in Del Mar, California; Mike and Sharon moved with their family to Whitefish, Montana; and Dan lives with his family in Boise.

Arlen & Derrel Crouch
1999 - present (2009)

By the time the Arlen and Derrel Crouch purchased Redfish Lake Lodge in 1999, it was one of the most popular vacation destinations in Idaho. It had become an Idaho icon. The Crouches began ownership determined to make the lodge one of the finest rustic resorts in the country, and they quickly undertook improvements and expansions towards that goal. Since acquiring Redfish Lake Lodge, they have made remarkable contributions, adding seven major buildings and a more permanent dock.

Arlen & Derrel Crouch

Arlen Crouch was born and raised in Jerome, Idaho. As a youth, he had many opportunities to visit the Stanley Basin and Redfish Lake Lodge. He visited it as a Boy Scout, as well as with his family. Most often, he and his father would visit alone, because the road over Galena made his mother nervous. Arlen recalls, "In those days [1940s] the road over Galena was a single lane dirt road. If you met another car coming in the opposite direction, one of you had to back up until you could find a wide spot in the road."[53] Arlen and his father were undaunted by the precarious travel, and on each trip they would stop at the present day Galena Lookout location, and his father would proclaim, "This is the greatest view on earth." Indeed, his father's proclamation rings literally true to Arlen, who has since traveled all over the world. He remains convinced there is no more beautiful place.

Arlen and his wife Derrel, also from Jerome, left their beloved Idaho as a young couple, and Arlen embarked on a successful career in financial investment and management. Though their business ventures and travels took them elsewhere, Idaho was not far from their minds, and they felt strongly loyal to their roots. Arlen often brought business associates to the Sawtooths, and "each time the beauty and the commitment of keeping the area as it was in [his] youth would impress [him]."[54] On one of these trips in the early 1990s, he heard that Redfish Lake Lodge was for sale, and he began exploring the business opportunity.

Arlen gathered his family together in Utah to discuss this unique business opportunity. He wanted it to be a family venture, and he asked each of his four children and their spouses if they were interested. Audra Crouch's husband Jeff Clegg was excited about the opportunity from the beginning. Jeff, also a native of Idaho, had a deep love for his home state. He had first visited Redfish Lake in his early twenties with his brother, and as they pulled into Redfish Lake, Jeff remembers thinking, "You gotta be kidding me. There's a place like this on earth?"[55] They only stayed for a few short hours, but the impression was significant. He even made a mental note that it would be a great place for a honeymoon, and sure enough, in 1989, he and Audra honeymooned in the present day Executive Cabin, which was then considered the honeymoon cabin.

Arlen and Derrel originally deferred the idea of purchasing the lodge, but it was still for sale in 1996, and they renewed their interest, with Jeff and Audra on board to manage the resort. With the help of business associate, Steve Thorsen, they began negotiating a sale with the See family. They struck a mutually agreeable deal in September of 1998. The legal documents were signed, the public review period ended without negative comment, and thus the Crouch family became official owners of Redfish Lake Lodge on January 4, 1999.

Jeff & Audra Clegg family

At the time of purchase, Arlen and Derrel were serving a three-year mission in Washington D.C. for the LDS church, so Jeff and Audra were solely responsible for the day-to-day management from the beginning. Jeff began working as a full-time employee of Redfish Lake Lodge, LLC in January 1999. Jack and Patty See helped with hiring the first season and recruited former employees to return and help in the transition to new ownership. Jeff and Audra spent the first couple of seasons familiarizing themselves with the lodge as a business. They undertook remodeling and refurbishing projects, like a new lobby floor and new bathroom floors in the lodge, but it wasn't until Arlen and Derrel returned from their mission that they launched their major improvement campaign.

Arlen and Derrel visited the lodge for the first time as owners in July 2000. Arlen was eager to begin significant building improvements to the resort and began meeting with the Forest Service to interpret the master plan and get approval for additional construction. They teamed up with architect Jack Smith from Sun Valley, Idaho, to embark on a building campaign that would result in a new, more permanent dock and seven new buildings within the following three years. The new buildings include four family-style Creekside Cabins, a Honeymoon Cabin, the two motel-style Kokanee Suites, and a modernized laundry facility. In addition, they have remodeled, restored, or refurbished nearly all of the existing cabins, and they have made significant investments improving unseen infrastructure, such as installing new water delivery and fire suppression systems, updating electrical systems, and removing dead and dying beetle infested trees.

The fundamental services offered remain the same, though with a distinctive touch. For example, they offer a sunset appetizer cruise on the lake and expanded menu options at the outdoor food and beverage gazebo. They also sponsor local Idahoan musicians for evening concerts on the front lawn and an annual mountain triathlon. They have also become a popular wedding destination, hosting weddings nearly every week of the open season.

As the Crouches and Cleggs operate and improve Redfish Lake Lodge on the principal of making it one of the finest rustic resorts in the country, they carry on Bob Limbert's vision of making Redfish ``the last word'' in resorts of its kind.

Timeline

8000 B.C.	Prehistoric hunters use the Redfish Rock Shelter.
1800s A.D.	Native American Sheepeater tribe inhabits the area.
1824	Alexander Ross leads fur trappers through Stanley Basin.
1860s	Prospectors and miners flood the region. Redfish Lake provides recreation for them, as well as sustenance from its bounty of fish.
1880s	Redfish Lake becomes a commercial destination, where fishermen harvest fish to sell to local restaurants and hotels. Talk of building a cannery is stymied by legislation prohibiting traps. The lake becomes a recreation destination for both Sawtooth and Wood River Valley residents.
1880 or 1881	Wagon road built over Galena Summit.
1905	President Teddy Roosevelt creates Sawtooth Forest Reserve. Congress changes name to Sawtooth National Forest in 1907.
1908	William and Lela Woolley homestead at Redfish Lake but leave by 1910.
1910s	Forest Service builds first trails, campgrounds, and picnic areas at the lake.
1911	Idaho residents, including Idaho Federation of Women's Clubs, propose park status for the Redfish Lake area.
1912	District Ranger W.H. Horton proposes protecting Redfish Lake from sheep grazing.
1913	Dick Horstman applies for homestead near Redfish Lake. Congressmen introduce bill to create Sawtooth National Park. Agricultural, mining, and timber advocates oppose the bill.
1915	Forest Service installs telephone at Redfish Lake. Occupancy Act of 1915 allows 30-year special use permits.
1919	Two miles of road constructed linking Redfish Lake with the highway.

1920s	Over-fishing leads to fish planting system in the region. Redfish Lake is the first to be planted. Grazing is prohibited around lake and timber-cutting is restricted.
1920s	Bob Limbert publicizes area through photographic essays.
1920	Road over Galena Summit is improved initiating first tourist boom to area. Bureau of Reclamation proposes using Redfish Lake as reservoir. Forest Service debates the idea. The idea is not officially withdrawn until 1972.
1920	Horstman receives permit to build Lake Hotel and boat rental business.
late-1920s	Limbert proposes constructing private summer cabins around lake. The Forest Service opposes the idea.
1926	Forest Service designates recreational and scenic value of Redfish Lake the primary consideration in land-use decisions.
1926	Limbert and six others form Sawtooth Tours, Inc. to develop tourism in the Sawtooths.
1927	Limbert partners with Horstman to lease commercial properties at Redfish Lake, except the boating concession.
1928	Limbert begins remodeling facilities at Redfish Lake with financial backing from Lewis Megowen and JL Kraft. At least two others apply for permits to develop on Redfish Lake.
1928	Idaho state constructs highway through Stanley Basin and Forest Service improves road from highway to Redfish.
1928	Dick Horstman dies in September.
1929	Megowen, Limbert's primary investor, loses all his money speculating on the stock market. Limbert courts new investors. He completes construction on gas station, 8 canvas tent cabins, dining room, and kitchen. He acquires the boating concession and achieves partial operation for the summer season, serving meals and operating two motorboats.
1931	Limbert completes construction of Redfish Lake facilities, including 3 duplex cabins. Brochure lists George S. Krom as manager.

1933	Bob Limbert dies of a heart attack in June. Lodge facilities apparently pass to George S. Krom.
c.1934	Brochure lists George S. Krom as contact with a NYC winter address.
1934-1941	Commercial status of Redfish Lake Lodge is unclear. It is reportedly open on and off. Some reports suggest that the lodge was closed but boats could still be rented.
1937-1940	Civilian Conservation Corps at Redfish Lake improves infrastructure like trails, roads, and campgrounds.
1941-1945	Lodge is closed during WWII and suffers vandalism.
1946	New owners Jess Worthington and Roy Butcher reopen lodge.
1953	Worthington and Butcher sell the lodge to Loran and Helen Olson, Pret and Sally Maughan, and Jay and Pearl Gorton.
1954	Gortons opt out of lodge ownership. Forest Service completes installation of power line. Lodge is wired for electricity.
1958	Forest Service begins era of major development at the lake and constructs Outlet and Point campgrounds, boat launch, and visitor center.
1959	Forest Service suggests creating a bar at the lodge but Olson and Maughan decline. Olson and Maughan sell to Redfish Lake Enterprises.
1960	National Park debate rekindles after Senator Frank Church proposes park status for Sawtooth region.
1960	Redfish Lake Enterprises begins ownership. Owners include Bob Coiner, Ken Brown, Mel Jensen, and Bob Tucker. Brown opts out shortly and Art Harshbarger enters the partnership. Owners begin construction of 40-space trailer court, remodel lodge to enclose the front porch and create a lobby area, add a porch the length of the lodge, and convert the original lobby area to a lounge.
1961	Owners build new store and move original store to become a rental cabin, and they dig a new well.

1962	Forest Service opens Redfish Lake Visitor's Center.
1965	Steven Coiner and Galen Tucker drown in canoeing accident.
c.1965	Owners build Pinerest rental unit and public laundry house and showers. They tap into newly installed Forest Service water system.
1966	Senator Len Jordan proposes National Recreation Area status for Sawtooth region.
1966	Lodgepole rental unit is constructed.
1969	Idaho state completes Highway 21 linking Boise area to Stanley.
1971	Redfish Lake Enterprises sells to Donald See family.
1972	Donald See family begins ownership with Jack and Patty See as managers. The original gas station is relocated and Forest Service constructs public restrooms in its place.
1972	The Sawtooth National Recreation Area is created.
1976	Manager's cabin is constructed from logs salvaged from a miner's cabin at Joe's Gulch near Lower Stanley.
1978	See family extends back of lodge creating more seating in dining room and more guest rooms upstairs. Kitchen is also extended 4 feet. A new gas station, public showers, and laundry facilities are constructed.
1979	Road access is rerouted to north and behind the lodge, rather than in front of it. Lodgepole rental unit is relocated to the present day location of Lake Suites to accommodate new road.
1980	Deluxe Cabins are constructed, replacing trailer court.
1981	Ice house is torn down.
1986	Lake Cabin is constructed as personal cabin for the See family but quickly becomes a rental unit.

1987	See family builds the Gazebo, Lake Suites, Fishhook Cabins, and Getaway Cabin and moves Lodgepole to its present location.
1989	Sees list Redfish Lake Lodge for sale in Wall Street Journal.
c1992	Sees remodel General Store.
1994	Sees add outside staircase to lodge.
1996	Arlen Crouch begins negotiations with See family to purchase lodge.
1998	Deal closes between Crouch and Sees.
1999	Arlen and Derrel Crouch begin ownership with Jeff and Audra Clegg as managers.
2000	Crouches launch website www.redfishlake.com.
2001	Crouches construct new docks built in a T-shape and more permanent than previous docks. They operate the first season with computerized reservations.
2002	Crouches build Creekside and Honeymoon Cabins.
2003	Crouches tear down housekeeping building and construct Kokanee Suites in its place. A modernized housekeeping and laundry facility is constructed across the driveway.
2006	Crouches remodel Rustic Cabins with full bathrooms, hardwood floors, and gas fireplaces, as well as an adjoining door between the duplex units.

Photographs

Redfish Lake, 2004

Car camping at Redfish Lake, c1920
Courtesy Edith Robertson

Redfish Lake docks, c1919
Courtesy Brett Woolley

Redfish Lake docks, c1927
Courtesy Boise State University Special Collections: Robert W. Limbert Collection

Lake Hotel, c1925
Courtesy Boise State University Special Collections: Robert W. Limbert Collection

Lodge construction, 1928
Courtesy Boise State University Special Collections: Robert W. Limbert Collection

Lodge construction, 1928
Courtesy Boise State University Special Collections: Robert W. Limbert Collection

Lodge construction, 1928
Courtesy Boise State University Special Collections: Robert W. Limbert Collection

Lodge construction, 1928
Courtesy Boise State University Special Collections: Robert W. Limbert Collection

Lodge construction, 1928
Courtesy Boise State University Special Collections: Robert W. Limbert Collection

Bob Limbert, c1928
Courtesy Boise State University Special Collections: Robert W. Limbert Collection

Gas Station construction, c1928
Courtesy Boise State University Special Collections: Robert W. Limbert Collection

Gas Station construction, c1928
Courtesy Boise State University Special Collections: Robert W. Limbert Collection

Construction, c1928
Courtesy Boise State University Special Collections: Robert W. Limbert Collection

Lodge construction, c1929
Courtesy Boise State University Special Collections: Robert W. Limbert Collection

Redfish Lake Lodge under construction, c1929
Courtesy Boise State University Special Collections: Robert W. Limbert Collection

George Blackman on right, first African-American resident of Custer County and carpenter at the lodge, c1928
Courtesy Boise State University Special Collections: Robert W. Limbert Collection

Redfish Lake docks, n.d.
Courtesy Boise State University Special Collections: Robert W. Limbert Collection

Redfish Lake docks, n.d.
Courtesy Redfish Lake Lodge collection

Redfish Lake docks, n.d.
Courtesy Boise State University Special Collections: Robert W. Limbert Collection

Redfish Lake beach, c1928
Courtesy Boise State University Special Collections: Robert W. Limbert Collection

Redfish Lake docks, c1928
Courtesy Boise State University Special Collections: Robert W. Limbert Collection

Tent cabin, c1929
Courtesy Boise State University Special Collections: Robert W. Limbert Collection

Road to Redfish Lake, c1933
Courtesy USFS

In "The Land of Tomorrow"

Redfish Lake Lodge, isolated in the heart of the Sawtooth National Forest Reserve, was built for the sportsman, horseback rider, camera hunter, naturalist and student; for the person who wants to turn his back on the grinding roar of the civilized world and seek the quiet and peace of this primitive untouched mountain country.

As yet modern man has not pushed into this rugged wilderness, dotted with hundreds of lakes, where altitudes range from 6,800 to 13,000 feet, almost the last outpost of a majestic, savage nature in the United States that remains untrammeled and unmarred.

Surprisingly close to the Lodge the hunter will find mountain goat, deer, elk, antelope, sheep and bear, while the fisherman can angle for trout of nearly every known variety, salmon or redfish, in nearby lakes and streams.

Endless strip-notch blazed trails of the U. S. Forestry Service stretch to all parts of this towering panorama to unfold heroic scenery and archaeological and geological specimens, little explored by the naturalist and scientist.

The Crater of the Moon Country, recently created a National Monument, where sixty-three extinct volcano craters rise skyward, still remains almost unknown.

Sixty miles from the railroad and eight from the nearest post office, Redfish Lake Lodge and cabins, built of native logs and timber, are of the mountains, but comfortable. The cabins have living room and private bath while each room in the Lodge has hot and cold running water. The food is of the best, but simple with an abundance of fresh vegetables, milk and cream from our own dairy. Mountain springs supply our unexcelled water.

Brochure, 1931
Courtesy Boise State University Special Collections: Robert W. Limbert Collection

Redfish Lake Lodge

Typical Double Cabin—each half accommodates three people and has its own fireplace.

Redfish Lake from Upper end, looking toward the Lodge.

Foot of Redfish Lake, with the rugged Sawtooth Range ascending from its shores. Taken from near Lodge.

Upper Redfish Lake, where it meets the foot of Mt. Heyburn . . . here you can climb 10,888 feet.

One hour's catch of Rainbow trout . . . all fish under 18 in. were thrown back.

Bob Limbert with an "honest fish story" about Salmon caught in the Salmon River.

Fishhook Creek . . . 2 miles from Redfish Lake Lodge . . . Mt. Heyburn on the left.

Brochure, 1931
Courtesy Boise State University Special Collections: Robert W. Limbert Collection

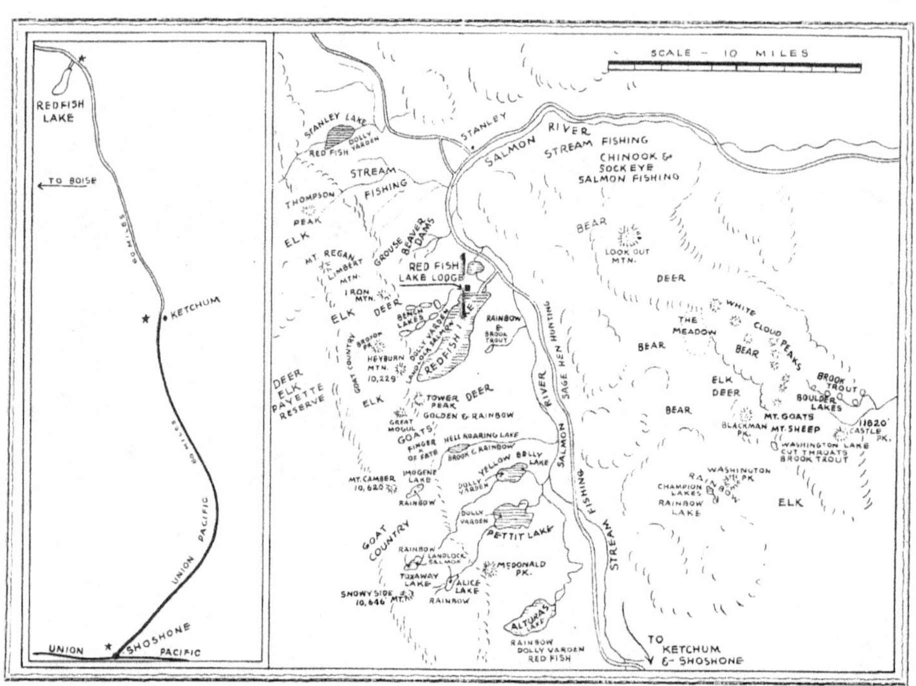

INFORMATION

SHOSHONE, IDAHO, is on the main line of the Union Pacific R. R. from Omaha, Nebraska, to Portland, Oregon—a branch of which extends to Ketchum—halfway to the Lodge.

Excellent automobile roads from Shoshone to Redfish Lake Lodge, through 120 miles of interesting and scenic country.

U. S. Forestry Telephone service to Hailey and Ketchum, Idaho. Telegraph address, Ketchum, Idaho.

Arrangements can be made for hunting, camping and exploration parties, with pack outfits and competent guides.

Bathing in the Lake—motor and row-boating, Mullins non-sinkable steel boats.

Guests will be met at either Ketchum or Shoshone upon 24 hour notice.

Redfish Lake Lodge is operated on the American plan. Rates including use of saddle horse 56 to 70 dollars per week per person.

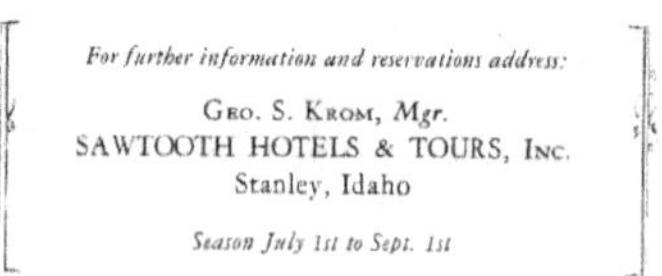

For further information and reservations address:

GEO. S. KROM, *Mgr.*
SAWTOOTH HOTELS & TOURS, INC.
Stanley, Idaho

Season July 1st to Sept. 1st

Brochure, 1931
Courtesy Boise State University Special Collections: Robert W. Limbert Collection

Rustic Cabins, built c1931, photo c2007

Redfish Lake Lodge, c1930
Courtesy Boise State University Special Collections: Robert W. Limbert Collection

Redfish Lake Lodge, c1931
Courtesy Boise State University Special Collections: Robert W. Limbert Collection

REDFISH LAKE LODGE

In the Heart of the

SAWTOOTH RANGE

STANLEY, IDAHO

Redfish Lake Lodge

Located at the headwaters of the main fork of the Salmon river, 60 miles north of Sun Valley,
isolated in the heart of the
SAWTOOTH NATIONAL FOREST RESERVE

The Lodge was built for the sportsman, horseback rider, camera hunter and naturalist, for the person who wants to turn his back on the grinding roar of the civilized world and seek quiet and peace in this untouched mountain country. One of the last outposts of a majestic wilderness in the United States, where altitudes range from 6,000 to over 13,000 feet and where there are hundreds of mountain lakes within a small area.

The fisherman can angle for trout, of nearly every known variety, salmon or redfish in nearby lakes and streams.

Blazed trails of the U. S. Forestry Service stretch to all parts of this towering panorama to unfold heroic scenery little explored. Arrangements can be made for pack trips.

There is a wide sandy beach sloping into the lake and the bathing and swimming are excellent. Mullins non sinkable steel rowboats and a motorboat provide transportation on five mile Redfish Lake.

Simple home cooking, with fresh vegetables, fruits, milk and cream.

Rooms in the Lodge have running hot and cold water. The cabins have 2 rooms and bath and fireplace.

Shoshone, Idaho, is on the main line of the Union Pacific R.R. from Omaha to Portland. Motor stage direct to Stanley meets the Monday, Wednesday and Friday train. The stage runs to Sun Valley daily and guests arriving upon the odd days will be met at Sun Valley upon 24 hrs. notice. By motor, route 93 runs within two miles of Redfish.

Redfish Lake Lodge is operated upon the American plan.

Rates upon application. Season June 15th to Sept. 15th.

For further information and reservations address:

GEORGE S. KROM
STANLEY, IDAHO

Oct. to June
151 East 80th St., N. Y. C.

Bridge at junction of Salmon River main fork, and Redfish Creek. Turn off route 93—Lake 2 miles

Typical cabin—each has living room, bedroom, bath and fireplace

MT. HEYBURN
(10,229 FEET)
As seen on approach

Brochure, c1934
Courtesy Jeff & Audra Clegg

Brochure, c1934
Courtesy Jeff & Audra Clegg

Redfish Lake Lodge, c1934
Courtesy Kelly Yost

Redfish Lake Lodge, c1934
Courtesy Kelly Yost

Dining room, c1934
Courtesy Kelly Yost

Lounge, c1934
Courtesy Kelly Yost

Emmett Hood family in front of boarded up lodge, 1935
Courtesy Emmett Hood

Emmett Hood family on Redfish Lake docks, 1935
Courtesy Emmett Hood

View from Redfish Lake Lodge, c1934
Courtesy Kelly Yost

Honeymooning couple at lodge, 1946
Courtesy Kelly Yost

Typical cabin — each has a living room, bedroom, bath and fireplace.

Section of the Dining Room in the Lodge.

View of the comfortable Lounge in the Lodge where the day's experiences are relived in the glow of hearth fire.

Located at the headwaters of the main fork of the Salmon River, 60 miles north of Sun Valley, isolated in the heart of the SAWTOOTH NATIONAL FOREST RESERVE.

Map shows the location of the Lodge only 2 miles from U.S. Highway 93—turn off Highway 93 just before the bridge at junction of Salmon River main fork and Redfish Creek.

For your comfort, modern conveniences are provided in rooms in the Lodge and in the cabins—hot and cold running water, electricity and modern plumbing. Rooms in the cabins are large and comfortably furnished. The grounds are well lighted.

The Lodge specializes in simple home cooking, with plenty of fresh vegetables, fruits, milk and cream. Pure, ice cold mountain spring water flows from your faucet.

Redfish Lake Lodge is operated upon the European Plan. Season is from June 1st through Oct. 15.

Rates: Rooms in Lodge—single $4.00 per day; double $5.00 per day.

Cabins—2 persons $6.00 each per day; 3 persons $5.00 each per day; 4 persons $4.50 each per day.

Dining Room in Lodge. Souvenirs & groceries in Trading Post.

For further information and reservation call or write:
RED FISH LAKE LODGE, STANLEY, IDAHO

Owners: PRET MAUGHAN, Mgr. & LORAN OLSON

Brochure, c1954
Courtesy Loran & Helen Olson

REDFISH LAKE LODG[E]
was built for the sportsman
nature lover, camera hunter
horseback rider and naturalis[t]
—for the person who want[s]
to turn his back upon th[e]
grinding roar of the civilize[d]
world and seek quiet an[d]
peace in this untouched mountain country. This is one o[f]
the last outposts of majesti[c]
wilderness in the Unite[d]
States, where altitudes range from 6,000 to over 13,000 fee[t]
and where there are hundreds of mountain lakes and streams
FISHING The fisherman can angle for trout of nearly ever[y]
known variety, salmon or redfish in nearby lakes and streams
NATURE LOVERS Blazed trails of the U. S. Forestry Service stretch to all parts of this towering panorama to unfol[d]
heroic scenery little explored. This primitive territory is [a]
National Forest and is not open to commercial development
CAMERA HUNTERS Here is scenery to delight the pho-
tographic eye—virgin forest, snow capped mountain peaks
mirroring lakes, rushing streams, sport action shots, wild game
pack trails, a wealth of nature studies.
HORSEBACK RIDING A string of good trail horses i[s]
stabled at the Lodge. Scenic pack trips can be arranged.
SWIMMING There is a wide sandy beach sloping into th[e]
lake and the bathing and swimming are excellent.
BOATING Mullins non-sinkable steel rowboats as well a[s]
motorboats are available. Five mile Redfish Lake is pronounce[d]
by world travelers as the world's most beautiful lake.

Brochure, c1954
Courtesy Loran & Helen Olson

"Redfish Lake," Postcard Collection--Lakes, c1950s
Courtesy Idaho State Historical Society Public Archives and Research Library

"Trading Post," Redfish Lake Collection, late 1950s
Courtesy Idaho State Historical Society Public Archives and Research Library

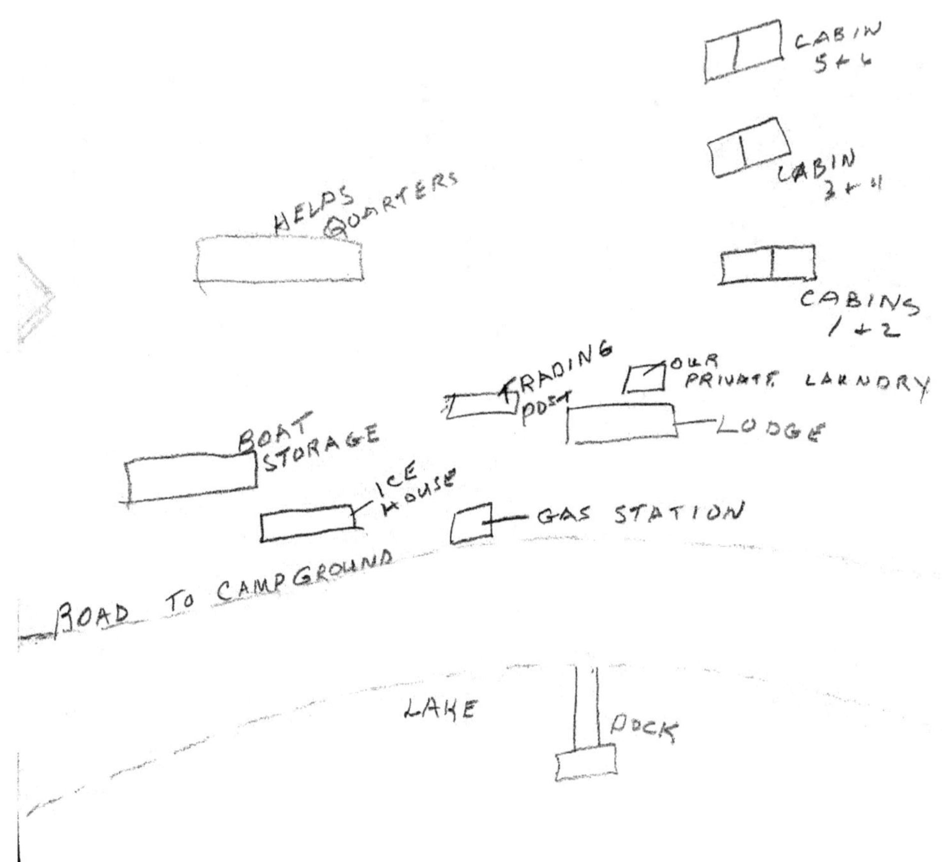

Redfish Lake Lodge map, 1954
Sketched by Helen Olson

Lodge, c1960
Courtesy Mel & Elva Jensen

RUSTIC LOUNGE
for your favorite cocktail

LODGE RESTUARANT
Relaxed, Informal Dining

TYPICAL CABIN
Livingroom
Bedroom
Bath & Fireplace

GENERAL STORE
Groceries
Fishing Tackle

TRAILER PARK
Lights
Water
Sewer

REDFISH LAKE LODGE

Located at the headwaters of the mainfork of the Salmon River, 60 miles north of Sun Valley. Isolated in the heart of the Sawtooth National Forest Reserve bordering Idaho's Primitive Area.

Map shows the location of the Lodge only 2 miles from U.S. Highway 93 -- turn off Highway 93 just before the bridge at junction of Salmon River main fork and Redfish Creek.

For your comfort, modern conveniences are provided in heated rooms in the Lodge and in the cabins--hot and cold running water, electricity and modern plumbing. Rooms in the cabins are large and comfortably furnished with fireplaces. The grounds are well lighted.

The Lodge maintains a Modern Trailer Park with space by day or week. Complete with lights, water and sewer.

The Lodge Restaurant offers an excellent, reasonably priced menu with a mountain atmosphere. You may enjoy your favorite cocktail in the "Rustic Lounge".

Our Service Station carries, Gas, Oil, Boating Equipment & Supplies.

The General Store carries, Fishing Equipment, Licenses, Camera Supplies, Souvenirs, Groceries, Ice and Cold Beer.

Season is from Memorial Day through Oct. 15. Special Spring Rates before June 20th and Special Fall Rates after Sept. 15th and during "Big Game Hunting Season".

Rates: Rooms in Lodge - Single $6.00 per day; Double $8.00. Extra bed $1.50.

Cabins -- 2 persons $6.00 each per day; 3 persons $5.00 each per day; 4 persons $4.50 each per day. We have one large Family Cabin available.

For further information and reservation call or write:
REDFISH LAKE LODGE, STANLEY, IDAHO

Owners: REDFISH LAKE ENTERPRISES, INC.
Manager: C.R. "Bob" Tucker
Winter Address: Box 751, Twin Falls, Idaho

REDFISH LAKE LODGE

Brochure, c1962
Courtesy Mel & Elva Jensen

REDFISH LAKE LODGE

REDFISH LAKE LODGE was built for the sportsman, nature lover, camera hunter, horseback rider and naturalist—for the person who wants to turn his back upon the grinding roar of the civilized world and seek quiet and peace in this untouched mountain country. This is one of the last outposts of majestic wilderness in the United States, where altitudes range from 6,000 to over 13,000 feet and where there are hundreds of mountain lakes and streams.

FISHING The fisherman can angle for trout of nearly every known variety, salmon or redfish in nearby lakes and streams.

NATURE LOVERS Blazed trails of the U. S. Forestry Service stretch to all parts of this towering panorama to unfold majestic scenery little explored. This primitive territory is a National Forest and is not open to commercial development.

CAMERA HUNTERS & ARTISTS Here is scenery to delight the eye—virgin forest, snow capped mountain peaks, mirroring lakes, rushing streams, sport action shots, wild game, pack trails, a wealth of nature studies.

HORSEBACK RIDING The Lodge's world famous "Alpine Ride" takes you into the breathtaking Beauty of Idaho's primitive area; a day never to be forgotten. Other scenic rides are equally enjoyable.

SWIMMING Directly in front of the Lodge there is a white sandy beach sloping into the Lake—Sun bathing and swimming are excellent. It is a safe area for children.

BOATING A variety of safe rowboats and motorboats are available. Water skiing and scenic boat trips. Five mile Redfish Lake is pronounced by world travelers as the world's most beautiful lake. Dock facilities and cement boat ramp for your convenience.

HUNTING The Sawtooth area provides excellent hunting for Elk, Deer, and Goat. Guide Service available—Inquire:

"STILL THE OLD WEST" Stanley, 5 miles from the Lodge, is a typical frontier town of the picturesque Old West.

Water Skiing at Red Fish Lake Lodge

Boat Dock in Front of Lodge

On the Alpine Ride

Brochure, c1962
Courtesy Mel & Elva Jensen

Maiden voyage of pontoon boat, Lady of the Lake, 1965
Courtesy Mel & Elva Jensen

Maiden voyage of pontoon boat, Lady of the Lake, 1965
Courtesy Mel & Elva Jensen

Lodge, c1960
Courtesy Mel & Elva Jensen

Cutting ice on the lake, early 1960s
Courtesy Mel & Elva Jensen

Cutting ice on the lake, 1960s
Courtesy Mel & Elva Jensen

Cutting ice on the lake, 1960s
Courtesy Mel & Elva Jensen

Ice House, c1960
Courtesy Mel & Elva Jensen

Ice House, c1960
Courtesy Mel & Elva Jensen

Shoveling snow off the lodge roof, c1960
Courtesy Mel & Elva Jensen

Winter at the lodge, c1960
Courtesy Mel & Elva Jensen

RUSTIC
LOUNGE
for your
favorite
cocktail

LODGE
RESTAURANT
Relaxed,
Informal
Dining

TYPICAL
CABIN
Living Room
Bedroom
Bath and
Fireplace

GENERAL
STORE
Groceries
Fishing Tackle
Souvenirs
Ice
Camp Supplies

TRAILER
PARK
Lights
Water
Sewer
Propane

REDFISH LAKE LODGE

Located at the headwaters of the main fork of the Salmon River, 60 miles north of Sun Valley, in the heart of the Sawtooth National Forest bordering the Sawtooth and Idaho Primitive Areas.

Map shows the location of the Lodge only 2 miles from U. S. Highway 93 — turn off Highway 93 just before the bridge at junction of Redfish Lake Creek and the main Salmon River.

ROOMS — Modern except private rest rooms - electric heat - comfortable.

CABINS — Each with 2 rooms, electric heat, fireplace, private rest room and shower.

MOTELS — Two new and very modern 4-plex motels also add to the accommodations available for you.

Well lighted grounds around the cabins and motels.

The Lodge maintains a Modern Trailer Park with space by day or week. Complete with lights, water and sewer.

The Lodge Restaurant offers an excellent, reasonably priced menu with a mountain atmosphere. You may enjoy your favorite cocktail in the "Rustic Lounge."

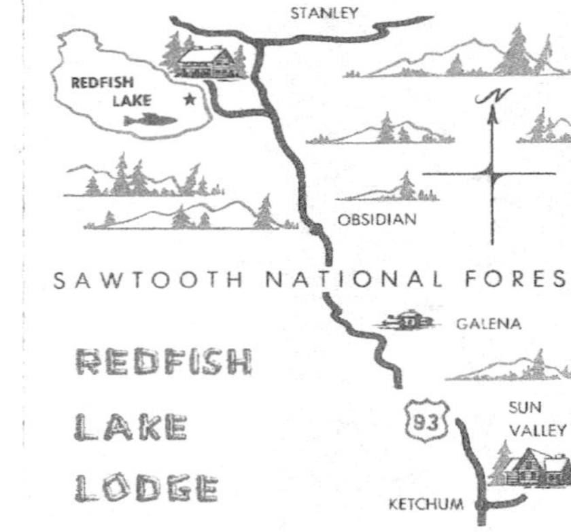

Our Service Station carries Gas, Oil, Boating Equipment, Supplies—Bar and Marina.

The General Store carries Fishing Equipment, Licenses, Camera Supplies, Souvenirs, Groceries, Ice and Cold Beer.

Season is from Memorial Day through October 15.

Rates: Rooms in Lodge - Single $9.50 per day; Double $10.50, Extra bed $1.50.

Cabins—2 persons $19.00 per day; 3 persons $20.50 per day; 4 persons $22.00 per day. We have one large Family Cabin available for 6 people (4 beds, 2 Double—2 Single @ $24.50. No fireplace in this unit.

Motels—2 people $19.00; 4 people $22.00.

PHONE - AREA CODE 208 - NUMBER 774-2836

For further information and reservation call or write:
REDFISH LAKE LODGE, STANLEY, IDAHO 83278

Owners: REDFISH LAKE ENTERPRISES, INC.
Manager: C. R. "Bob" Tucker
Winter Address: Box 751, Twin Falls, Idaho 83301

Brochure, late 1960s
Courtesy Mel & Elva Jensen

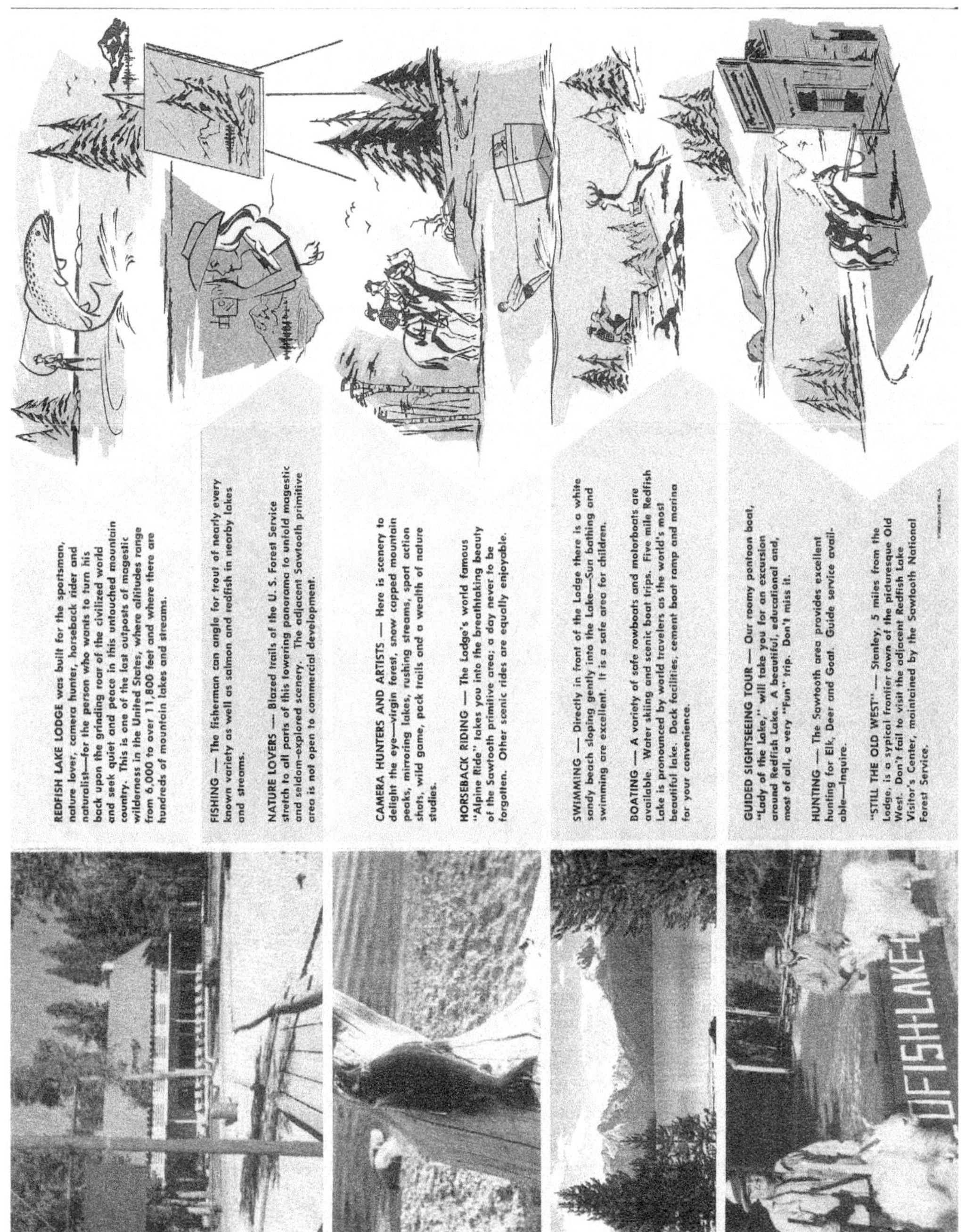

REDFISH LAKE LODGE was built for the sportsman, nature lover, camera hunter, horseback rider and naturalist—for the person who wants to turn his back upon the grinding roar of the civilized world and seek quiet and peace in this untouched mountain country. This is one of the last outposts of magestic wilderness in the United States, where altitudes range from 6,000 to over 11,800 feet and where there are hundreds of mountain lakes and streams.

FISHING — The fisherman can angle for trout of nearly every known variety as well as salmon and redfish in nearby lakes and streams.

NATURE LOVERS — Blazed trails of the U. S. Forest Service stretch to all parts of this towering panorama to unfold magestic and seldom-explored scenery. The adjacent Sawtooth primitive area is not open to commercial development.

CAMERA HUNTERS AND ARTISTS — Here is scenery to delight the eye—virgin forest, snow capped mountain peaks, mirroring lakes, rushing streams, sport action shots, wild game, pack trails and a wealth of nature studies.

HORSEBACK RIDING — The Lodge's world famous "Alpine Ride" takes you into the breathtaking beauty of the Sawtooth primitive area; a day never to be forgotten. Other scenic rides are equally enjoyable.

SWIMMING — Directly in front of the Lodge there is a white sandy beach sloping gently into the Lake—Sun bathing and swimming are excellent. It is a safe area for children.

BOATING — A variety of safe rowboats and motorboats are available. Water skiing and scenic boat trips. Five mile Redfish Lake is pronounced by world travelers as the world's most beautiful lake. Dock facilities, cement boat ramp and marina for your convenience.

GUIDED SIGHTSEEING TOUR — Our roomy pontoon boat, "Lady of the Lake," will take you for an excursion around Redfish Lake. A beautiful, educational and, most of all, a very "Fun" trip. Don't miss it.

HUNTING — The Sawtooth area provides excellent hunting for Elk, Deer and Goat. Guide service available—Inquire.

"STILL THE OLD WEST" — Stanley, 5 miles from the Lodge, is a sypical frontier town of the picturesque Old West. Don't fail to visit the adjacent Redfish Lake Visitor's Center, maintained by the Sawtooth National Forest Service.

Brochure, late 1960s
Courtesy Mel & Elva Jensen

Road in front of lodge, 1960s
Courtesy Josh Johnson

Sailboat regatta, 1960s
Courtesy Josh Johnson

Trailer court, early 1960s
Courtesy Josh Johnson

Trailer court, early 1960s
Courtesy Josh Johnson

Trailer court, early 1960s
Courtesy Josh Johnson

General Store, c1961
Courtesy Josh Johnson

Pinerest motel built c1965, photo 2004

Paddleboats, c1972
Courtesy Josh Johnson

Paddleboats, c1972
Courtesy Mel & Elva Jensen

Lodge, c1972
Courtesy Jack & Patty See

TYPICAL CABIN
Livingroom
Bedroom
Bath
Fireplace

LODGE RESTAURANT
Relaxed,
Informal
Dining

TYPICAL LODGE ROOM
Log Built
Wash Basin
Community Bath

RUSTIC LOUNGE
for your
favorite
cocktail

HORSEBACK RIDING
World Famous Alpine Ride
Overnite Mountain Lake Fishing Trip
Shorter Scenic Tours

REDFISH LAKE LODGE

Located at the headwaters of the main fork of the Salmon River, 60 miles north of Sun Valley, in the heart of the Sawtooth National Forest, bordering the Sawtooth wilderness area.

Map shows the location of the Lodge only 2 miles from U.S. Highway 75 — turn off Highway 75 at the bridge at junction of Redfish Lake Creek and the main Salmon River.

ROOMS — Comfortable electric heat. Community bath in Lodge.

CABINS — Each with 2 rooms, electric heat, fireplace, private bath.

MOTELS — Two motels also add to the accommodations available for you.

Well lighted grounds around the cabins and motels.

The Lodge Restaurant offers an excellent, reasonably priced menu with a mountain atmosphere. You may enjoy your favorite cocktail in the "Rustic Lounge."

STANLEY
LOWMAN
HWY 21
REDFISH LAKE LODGE
HWY 75
IDAHO CITY
BOISE
SUN VALLEY
HWY 20
FAIRFIELD
I-84
MOUNTAIN HOME
TWIN FALLS

Our Service Station carries Gas, Oil, Boating Equipment and Supplies. We also have Marina, Laundromat, Horses, Ice and Public Showers. The General Store carries Fishing Equipment, Licenses, Camera Supplies, Souvenirs, Groceries and Cold Beer.

Let us smoke your fish with true mountain hickory flavor. Season is from Memorial Day through October 5.

PHONE — 208/774-3536

For further information and reservation call or write:

REDFISH LAKE LODGE, STANLEY, IDAHO 83278

Owners: REDFISH LAKE LODGE, Inc.

Managers: Jack and Patty See, Mike and Sharon Poehling

Brochure, c1980
Courtesy Jack & Patty See

Brochure, c1980
Courtesy Jack & Patty See

Lodge, c1972
Courtesy Jack & Patty See

Original gas station, 1972
Courtesy Jack & Patty See

Docks, early 1970s
Courtesy Jack & Patty See

Docks, mid 1970s
Courtesy Jack & Patty See

Lodge, mid 1970s
Courtesy Jack & Patty See

Winter scene, 1970s
Courtesy Jack & Patty See

Winter scene, 1970s
Courtesy Jack & Patty See

Winter scene, 1970s
Courtesy Jack & Patty See

Winter scene, 1970s
Courtesy Jack & Patty See

Addition to lodge, 1979
Courtesy Jack & Patty See

Addition to lodge, 1979
Courtesy Jack & Patty See

Addition to lodge, 1979
Courtesy Jack & Patty See

Lodge, c1987
Courtesy Jack & Patty See

Lodge, 1980s
Courtesy Jack &Patty See

General Store, c1979
Courtesy Jack & Patty See

General Store remodel, c1992
Courtesy Jack & Patty See

General Store remodel, c1992
Courtesy Jack & Patty See

Gazebo, constructed 1978
Courtesy Jack & Patty See

Forest Service public restrooms, c1972
Courtesy Jack & Patty See

Managers cabin, 1976
Courtesy Jack & Patty See

Public showers and laundry construction, 1978
Courtesy Jack & Patty See

Fishhook Cabin built 1987, photo 2004

Deluxe Cabins built 1980, photo 2004

Lake Suites built 1987, photo 2004

Getaway Cabin built 1987, photo 2004

Lake Cabin built 1986, photo 2004

Picture yourself:

- Dropping a line in one of hundreds of mountain lakes and streams, home to salmon and nearly every variety of trout.
- Boating, canoeing, kayaking, water-skiing, or swimming in picturesque Redfish Lake, known by seasoned travelers as the world's most beautiful lake. Or enjoying its natural beauty at a leisurely pace on an excursion aboard "Lady of the Lake," our spacious pontoon boat. We also offer a shuttle service across the lake to the Transfer Camp. This shuttle saves 6 miles for backpackers and day hikers.
- Taking the World Famous Alpine Ride through the breathtaking Sawtooth Wilderness Area on horseback. Or exploring any number of established trails on foot or bicycle.
- Capturing the backdrop of dense forests, snow-capped mountain peaks, and mirroring lakes on film or canvas.

Guests are welcome to plan their own activities or ask our trained, professional staff to arrange guides and tour services.

P.O. Box 9
Redfish Lake Lodge
Stanley, Idaho 83278

Brochure, 2001

Brochure, 2001

Sign at turnoff for the lodge, 2004

Lodge, 2004

Docks, 2004

Docks, 2004

View from lodge to docks, 2004

Sailboat on Redfish Lake, 2004

General Store, 2004

Service Station, 2004

Redfish Corrals, 2004

Gazebo, 2004

Creekside Cabin, 2004

Honeymoon Cabin, 2004

Kokanee Suite, 2004

Dining room, 2004

Rustic Lounge, 2004

Lodge, 2004

Acknowledgments

I gratefully acknowledge the many people who assisted with this project. Thanks to Margaret Lawrence who donated her father's documents, letters, and photographs to the Boise State University Special Collections Library. I researched this collection for information on Bob Limbert's establishment of the lodge. In addition, I relied on a Clark T. Heglar's booklet, ``Redfish Lake Lodge: A Look at the Early History." The U.S. Forest Service has several historical reports which provided invaluable information: "Redfish Lake Lodge Historic District Site Evaluation" by Roshanna Stone and Richa Wilson; "Report on Navigability, Title, and Historic Use of Redfish Lake" by Matthew Godfrey; and "Big Redfish Lake, A Navigability History" by James Muhn and Susan Stacy. Beyond these documents, I relied on newspaper clippings, oral histories, brochures, and photographs from the Idaho State Historical Society Public Archives and Research Library and the Idaho Oral History Center. Most importantly, I have had the pleasure and honor of personal interviews and correspondence with the following former owners and associates of Redfish Lake Lodge: Margaret Lawrence, Kelly Yost, Sally Maughan, Loran and Helen Olson, Mel Jensen, Bob and Betty Coiner, Art Harshbarger, Jack and Patty See, Sharon Poehling, Jeff and Audra Clegg, and Arlen Crouch.

Special thanks to each of the following who shared information, memories, and photographs with me: Betty Rember, Jack Niece, Emmett Hood, Dean Rowland, Ilene Burr, Tom Wilkins, Josh Johnson, and Melinda Pride. Special thanks also to Kathy Hodges of the Idaho State Historical Society Public Archives, Jamie Bennett of the Sawtooth National Forest, and the staff at the Boise State University Special Collections Library. More special thanks to Steve Wursta for sharing so many photographs and his inspiring documentary, *The History of Redfish Lake Lodge*. Thanks to Amy Bankhead for the final edit. Thank you to my husband, without whose support and encouragement I never would have finished this project. Last, but not least, thank you to Arlen Crouch and Jeff Clegg for the financial and moral support that made publishing possible!

Kelsey Newman Benac

Bibliography

Boise State University Special Collections. Robert W. Limbert Collection. *Various letters, photographs, contracts, brochures, regional descriptions, and business proposals.* MSS 80 Box 1 Folders 3, 4, 6, 25, 33, and 70. MSS 80 Box 2 Folders 14, 17, 25, 33. Boise, Idaho.

D'Easum, Dick. *Sawtooth Tales.* Caldwell, Idaho: Caxton Printers Ltd., 1977.

Heglar, Clark T. *Redfish Lake Lodge: A Look at the Early History.* Star, Idaho: Porchswing Productions, nd.

The History of Idaho's Redfish Lake Lodge. By Steve Wursta. Arctic Circle Productions, 2006. DVD.

Idaho Oral History Center. *Various recorded interviews.* Boise, Idaho.

Idaho State Historical Society Public Archives and Research Library. *Various newspaper articles and photographs.* Boise, Idaho.

State of Idaho. *Big Redfish Lake: A Navigability History*, by James Muhn and Susan Stacy. March 20, 2003.

U.S. Forest Service. Sawtooth National Forest. *IMACS Site Form (USFS R4-2300-2, 4/89), Report No: SW-98-1893*, recorded by L.Mauser. August 13, 1998.

U.S. Forest Service. Sawtooth National Forest. *Redfish Lake Lodge Historic District Site SW-1446 (10CR1504) Evaluation*, by Roshanna Stone and Richa Wilson. Oct 24, 2001.

U.S. Forest Service. Sawtooth National Forest. *Report on Navigability, Title, and Historic Uses of Redfish Lake*, Godfrey, Matthew. Bothell, WA: Foster Wheeler Environmental Corp, March 26, 2003.

Yarber, Esther. *Stanley-Sawtooth Country.* Salt Lake City, Utah: Publishers Press, 1976.

Endnotes

1 Pride, Melinda, email to author, July 2002.

2 Kosich, Steven, email to author, May 2003.

3 Yarber, Esther, Stanley-Sawtooth Country (Salt Lake City, Utah: Publishers Press, 1976), 76.

4 U.S. Forest Service, Sawtooth National Forest, Report on Navigability, Title, and Historic Uses of Redfish Lake, by Matthew Godfrey, (Bothell, WA: Foster Wheeler Environmental Corp, March 26, 2003), 7.

5 Ibid., 10-11.

6 Ball, Peter, "An Easterner Sees the Sawtooths," Idaho Statesman, Aug 11, 1935. Idaho State Historical Society Public Archives and Research Library.

7 Limbert, Robert W., letter to Judge Shanks, Sep. 4, 1929. Boise State University Special Collections: Robert W. Limbert Collection.

8 For more detail on these years see Chapter ``George S. Krom."

9 Description current as of 2009.

10 For more detail on these years see Chapter ``George S. Krom."

11 State of Idaho, Big Redfish Lake: A Navigability History, by James Muhn and Susan Stacy, (2003), 14.

12 See, Jack and Patty, interview by author, Stanley, ID, Nov 4 2003.

13 Yarber, 193; U.S. Forest Service, Report on Navigability, Title, and Historic Uses of Redfish Lake, 21.

14 McGown, Edna, recorded interview by Glenn Oakley, March 16, 1983, 4. Idaho Oral History Center.

15 Rutledge, R.H., letter to Harry Falk, Dec 29, 1927. Boise State University Special Collections: Robert W. Limbert Collection.

16 Limbert, Robert W., letter to J.L. Kraft, May 23, 1928. Boise State University Special Collections: Robert W. Limbert Collection.

17 Limbert, Robert W., regional description and business proposal for Maryland Casualty Company, 3. Boise State University Special Collections: Robert W. Limbert Collection.

18 "Idaho Mountains Will be Exploited and Developed to Attract Tourists," Caldwell Tribune, Jan 14, 1927. Idaho State Historical Society Public Archives and Research Library.

19 Limbert, Robert W., letter to Lewis E. Megowen, July 18, 1928. Boise State University Special Collections: Robert W. Limbert Collection.

20 The History of Idaho's Redfish Lake Lodge, DVD, by Steve Wursta (Arctic Circle Productions, 2006).

21 Limbert, Robert W., letter to Donald Hough, July 15, 1928. Boise State University Special Collections: Robert W. Limbert Collection.

22 Limbert, Robert W., letter to E.C. Proctor, June 16, 1929. Boise State University Special Collections: Robert W. Limbert Collection.

23 Limbert, Robert W., letter to Clifford Beegle, June 21, 1929. Boise State University Special Collections: Robert W. Limbert Collection.

24 Limbert, Robert W., letter to Judge Shanks, September 4, 1929. Boise State University Special Collections: Robert W. Limbert Collection.

25 Limbert's desired patrons were wealthy Easterners, men in particular, because his business interest was multiple-day hunting and back country tours with the lodge as a base camp. Margaret Lawrence, Limbert's daughter, remembers "wealthy men" at the lodge but not women and children.

26 Lawrence, Margaret, interview by author, Boise, ID, Feb 27, 2003.

27 Wursta, Steve, email to author, January 2009.

28 Lawrence.

29 In Stanley-Sawtooth Country, Esther Yarber claims that the buildings and boats at Redfish were sold to George S. Krom. p 205.

30 Limbert, Robert W., letter to Judge Shanks, September 4, 1929. Boise State University Special Collections: Robert W. Limbert Collection.

31 U.S. Forest Service, Sawtooth National Forest, Redfish Lake Lodge Historic District Site SW-1446 (10CR1504) Evaluation, by Roshanna Stone and Richa Wilson, (Oct 24, 2001), 3.

32 The History of Idaho's Redfish Lake Lodge.

33 Hood, Emmett, letter to author, April 14, 2004.

34 U.S. Forest Service, Report on Navigability, Title, and Historic Uses of Redfish Lake, 28.

35 Niece, Jack, telephone interview with author, December 10, 2003.

36 Yost, Kelly, interview with author, Twin Falls, ID, March 20, 2003.

37 Burr, Irene Wells, telephone interview with author, April 12, 2004.

38 Ibid.

39 Rowland, Dean, letter to author, April 23, 2003.

40 Olson, Loran and Helen, interview with author, Boise, ID, January 9, 2004.

41 Ibid.

42 Ibid.

43 Maughan, Sally, interview with author, Boise, ID, January 9, 2004; Olson.

44 Maughan, Sally; U.S. Forest Service, Redfish Lake Lodge Historic District Site SW-1446 (10CR1504) Evaluation, 3.

45 Wilkins, Tom, email to author, December 2003.

46 Coiner, Bob and Betty, interview with author, Twin Falls, ID, February 18, 2003.

47 Wilkins.

48 "Sawtooth Valley Facelifting Shows up in Changes Made to Two Lodges," Times-News, July 24, 1960. Mel & Elva Jensen collection.

49 See.

50 Ibid.

51 Ibid.

52 Associated Press, "Redfish Lake Lodge For Sale," Idaho Statesman, Aug 2, 1989. Jeff & Audra Clegg collection.

53 Crouch, Arlen, letter to author, 2004.

54 Ibid.

55 Clegg, Jeff and Audra, interview with author, Jerome, ID, February 2004.

www.ingramcontent.com/pod-product-compliance
Lightning Source LLC
LaVergne TN
LVHW061223100826
845148LV00004B/837

9780578027920